See It Through

Merie Vision Publishing, LLC
www.merievisionpublishing.com

ISBN: 978-1-961213-08-1
Library of Congress Control Number on record

First Print Edition: May 2024

Love
in its
purest
Forms

Love
in its
purest
Forms

love
in its
purest
Forms

Mama, why do you love me so?

I love your little brown fro.

I love how your big brown eyes glow.

I love each and every one of your piggy wiggly ♡ toes. ♡

Mama loves how you say, ♡ "Hel-wo." ♡

Mama, why do you love me so?

Because I love the love you show.

I love how your
smile grows.

I love the cute way you say, "O."

I love when I give
you kisses, and you
say,
"Give me Mo'! Give
me Mo'!"

Mama, why do you love me so?

I love how you are always on the go.

I **love** how you like to whisper secrets really low.

I love the little

bubbles you blow.

I love how you are learning to walk. You're such a pro!

So, why does Mama love you so?

Because it's pure love that will ever continue to grow!!